SKY FOR A FOREIGN BIRD

Poetry and Poetry Translations

Fethi Sassi

Edited by Tendai Rinos Mwanaka
Typeset by Tendai R Mwanaka

Mwanaka Media and Publishing Pvt Ltd,
Chitungwiza Zimbabwe

*

Creativity, Wisdom and Beauty

Publisher: Tendai R Mwanaka

Mwanaka Media and Publishing Pvt Ltd *(Mmap)*

24 Svosve Road, Zengeza 1

Chitungwiza Zimbabwe

mwanaka@yahoo.com

www.africanbookscollective.com/publishers/mwanaka-media-and-publishing

https://facebook.com/MwanakaMediaAndPublishing/

Distributed in and outside N. America by African Books Collective

orders@africanbookscollective.com

www.africanbookscollective.com

ISBN: 978-1-77906-513-1

EAN:9781779065131

DISCLAIMER

All views expressed in this publication are those of the author and do not necessarily reflect the views of *Mmap*.

iii

Dedication

And you are raining too, o... my passion, my wonderful life.

APOLINAIRE

Table of Contents

Foreword

Fethi Sassi is a high flying poet hung in a sweet wetted cloud. He never hesitates to treat deep poetic texts with utmost love and happiness.

We can see that while other poets fly shy of treating such themes that are potentially deep. Really, he courageously treats them in this poetic paradise with a big soft touch to ensure lovers dance in front of the door of this wonderful world .He remains absolutely impartial and offera faithful view to the sky not full of stars but with plenty dreams, never to end and never to begin

Some of the poems in this collection are translations from Arabic as his original language, from which you can read this book in French,from English and from Persian, and other languages. *A sky for a Foreign Bird* emerges as pioneering work of romance .This poet gives for his lovely readers a graphic picture of a hug and kisses never to end and never stopped!

Poems

Flutes ache

"I'm a bad writer, sometimes even bad writers say the truth"
(Charles Bukowski)

Indeed;
I 'm not aspiring to the eternity,
but the fact of the matter is that, I reprimand the wind
at the opening of the poem.
I roister as god does in the poets' funeral.
I lie down on the brink of the tree which embraces
baby fruits.
Thus, I embroider my face on my shoulder and,
scatter climates for nostalgia.
In order to suckle the whims from a bundle of speech,
so, would the milk cry from the breast of the tale.
A dream lost on the sly with peeps star,
I have no face to wet my confusion in a sky
for a new happiness.
I will seclude myself in the bottom of the absence
scratch its sumptuous night.
Threatening the silence with the resignation of the emptiness;

and collect gravel to flirt the flutes' ache.

A wild woman

I say
Why don't I leave to the maze?
Laden with the winter,
Lost in the realm of poem.
That's why my mother told me:
Don't drink milk with jerks.
Ride towards the north of the night....
And drink her face...
No shadow left you; but what befalls you,
is the alienation of exiles upon the last cloud;
that splintered in the tavern of the night.

Indeed....
You desire nothing but a wild woman;
bones of a tree changing its clothes,
for your forthcoming wedding.
And a poem that wets the hair of water with a ballad,
thus we have parted like a hug....
Therefore, you have to flirt your wound my son,
pick up amazement from her lips.
Come in and let the sun wash her face in your hands...

Let the coal of the story blaze with your longing.
Dwell in the fire to warm up the poem in the shadow of elements.
Definitely the lightening will dwell stealthily in her cup of coffee.
So you become...
A stature of roses.. and a tavern of tears.
Then at the extremity of the poetry threads,
bathe in the salt of her lips.
Set the absence on fire….
To let the rose grow up with her bleeding fragrance,
and the poem issneaking on my fingertips .
The evening smells the metaphor,
excessive in counting its fingertips .
The spikes yearn for the call....
And the story remains like a tattoo on the shoulder of doves.....

She used to tell me

No blue except the color of the sea in your eyes;
She used to tell me…..

Whenever the night lights my fingers;
I put a blond star on your lips,
so the shadow grows up overtly.
Storms from my perfume.
She used to tell me…:

Your eyes are the way to the lusted sin;
opening the doors of eternities to me,
until the cloud takes shower on my tresses.
Draws on the branches of wind a moon from my waiting femininity;
and arched lips like a mystic rose from the rain horses.
he used to tell me…. :

I' m your female…. I still love you in spite of
the confusion of elements inside me.
Take whatever you like from my blood;
I'm now a cloud and you became a prophet.

I'm your female… wet with obedience, prostrate between your
letters.
So don't approach my colors,
this is my waist, your eternal bar.
In order that love picks the more beauty of my names.

Your female…. I'm,
desire of devil, east perfume is my waist.
So don't leave my happiness.
We are still on the poem stature,
Sharing love and absence.
………………………
She used to tell me….:

Flying like love, coming to my cities,
wearing the clay, wearing the losses.
You're oppressive;
wielding your night to the face of a song;
and you cry lonely in the waiting.
I will rain elegant drizzles on your lips.
Indeed, we are a mixture of mud and dreams.
Don't enter my night lonely,
and don't recommend the darkness.
I'm still hanging the lights in the mud.
No blue only the love color in your eyes.
She used to tell me.

Lover till the last line

I would like to give you a piece of advice;
and perhaps you will forget....
But you should not forget the sigh of a bare star,
between your fingers as a lover's will till the last cloud.
You have to write to the last line,
and put a full stop at the end of every dusk.
Yes...... thus you can prove your ability to forget...
For example you forgot the dawn lines hanging,
on the balcony of your little dreams,
as if they are playing with silence in a moving hall,
you have to forget the wave memory....
But pay attention;
while you are sinking; take a butterfly,
put on the back of the poem a burning idea,
and don't hide the errors of moon....
By wetting your lips from love jars.
Till the perfume of identification scorch you.....
But I see you suffering alone with a memory, that hurts you,
as if you have committed a sin.
There is nothing burning except the color of your cheek,
When a cloud embroiders your face, it turns off by crying.

As a night

She hasn't left....
But she reproaches her toothbrush for crying,
and for the time glasses,
she arranged her face from the features of absence,
afraid of leaving her memory on the table;
love is lying on a sofa made from the moon cough......
She said :
Who has planted a cloud in the night of my loneliness?
So it rained a volley of questions on my body.
The violins which are listening to the dusk of my loneliness,
are washing by the wine of your colors,
then to be combed overtly from my waiting waist;
only absence.....

Kisses you, to forget your face on a cloud,
and you leave as if you have an appointment
with the most beautiful losses,
perhaps you are preparing an everlasting rest,
for a forthcoming appointment.....
You carry the burden of absence, and on your shoulder;
a tattoo lost the key of its failure on poem lips,
like a star broke out in sweat in a moment of shame.
Why you learn an exile song by heart like poetry?
And you scream:
Hey.... rose, you perfumed the way of our loneliness;
and gave us the lily of seduction.

I'll wear a tree, and wave with branches to all the stars;
to turn green the stone face....
And the water laughs at the whinny of the story,
I.... I try to perceive your beautiful night,
but I haven't succeeded to wear your absence,
so don't dwell in my body.

"Bordet " lover

Prostrate;o…. long haired and dew.
Wash your feet with my tears.
Just wobble like a lazy lip,
and don't care about anything,
Just go around (the kaaba) of absence, only my face there
take a shower with the saliva of the beginnings….
Madam, do you know that the spring is coming!!
so don't let the moon travel alone…..
On the outskirts of metaphor as a shame night.
Sit down ….
This night doesn't know you,
with a flock of clouds on your face balcony;
gathering nostalgia….
when the sun passes, kiss it;
because I wrote a poem on its cheek.
The twilight goes back home early, before the sky of fingers sleep…
So, don't l let your night in the face of dreams,
and bind your laugh with the wind ropes.
You … "Bordet "of the lover who just came from a high travel….

and this sky is your pike from the rose clay.
Suckles the dust of maze.
So, we will sly the wind,
and we forget the grapes wound in the middle of the dream…

A poem continues in the ache

If only he…..
Was a poet tromping the words.
and between his arms clutters stutters,
fall in the deep of the absence
his fingers was wet as a night on the lips place….
Usually…..
He was relieving the moon if he sweats in the whiteness,
Than the sun stumbles in the braids reveal,
He was every night inventing for the sky two lips,
to kiss doves….
While…..
His dreams as a unseen needle sews,
two mustaches in the trope,
so far with pelican mummified in the rivers of the distance;
as he is…..

a butterfly wets her wings with the call
doesn't care if the sun raised in the maze night,
like this;
he washes the argil the letters of the poem,
and wets the salt hanged in the mouth of the wave,
running away from his face….
So that doesn't injure the wind.
He was everlasting the bewilderment….

Roving as a sun nipples…..
Hollowing as an emergent sadness.
With a poem continues in the ache,
Usually ....
He raves and says with a voice
returning from a long travel.
O….. lovers crowned of me.
Slave like a poem fingers,
come to me satisfied,
And enter in my dispersion,
dissolve in my blood…
and he shuts up.

I don't remember well…it was something like her face

She was drinking the rainbow…
Hiding behind the bottle of absence.
I don't remember well... but it was something like her face.
I was with her drinking my loneliness;
upon the arm of an apologizing flute...
But the night revealed to her its fragrance.
And invited her to sleep on the note of love...
Her face blazed with poetry; she melted as a poem.
She is still, as usual, looking from the window of time.
Like a butterfly between its fingertips a sob digging the memory...
Thus, names dangle for her like desperate bunches
on the walls of a poem.
That's why...
I don't leave her dream early,
until I choose the stones of oblivion to the wind .
I sleep with her, and on the hand of the evening a kiss hangs like
dreams of a kitten.
A lip shedding clouds that fall in the groves of amazement.
I will steal a star and hide amid the dust of words.
So, the night climbs alone the ladder of time,
chatting with an astonishing butterfly.
At the window of my heart,

I weave climates to the forthcoming seasons.
So, spread in the emptiness a song to me...
Kiss me! Your saliva is enough for me to drown.
You are the absent face from my poems.
Open the sun gate to me, to drink my storm,
because I see behind the absence a raining cloud;
upon her tearless cup of coffee,
like the hurting sunset smile.
Like the evening tale.
So be lenient waves!!
My fingertips care about her absence.
Her kiss is a whole poem.
Let's enter together the dungeons of her body.
There we shall knead the clay of the story;
venture in the folds of her charm.
And we never care about the chemistry of kisses...
But I don't remember well... It was something like her face.

The color of her eyes has another story

The cloud has a balcony overlooking the wind.
Imagine that the earth were sterile.
So it would not give birth to the probabilities of the beginning.
I play with the Sassoon in my fingers when you come;
before the cloud by half rose.
I came like the dichotomy of the dream in the range face,
but I explode your kiss, to make a cigarette from the clay.
And from the twilight passing on your cheek, a last colors brush,
in the hope of shutting down all the exists to the dream.
Then I comb my fingers to stay alone.
I arrange my tears according to my will.
Indeed, I didn't cry, but the color of your eyes has another story.
The language got old, and the berry's leaves have left.
I was sad, but I didn't peel the wind between your hands.
As if I wrote a poem and wore the tears.

So, when would poems and women leave me?
I,
I have a tent in the question's roots.
And a pub in its face that is patronized by lovers.
I have a winter on the beach of her eyes,
waiting for me, and other things.
I left my face on the carpet, and fell asleep like a strange night.

I wished then to die, and leave a speech to the coming storm,
as an arrogant wound,
or a night without questions.
I haven't committed an affront in the tradition of lovers.
But bunches have silent moments.
I was yelling;
and berating the wind when I found you in the stones' books,
a tyrannical star in the sky.
So let me rub your perfume with the clay of my eagerness.
I was improvising to reduce the absence;
who had poured the sad night into your eyes?
So, the stars seemed sad since the god dawn.
I was like that.
Kindling the wind with laughs and cry ...

Don't leave this poem in the hands of lovers

While you resist your beautiful laugh,
think well in the wide silence....
In the loose shirt of the unknown as my dreams.
Write something...
Or practice the narcissism of whiteness.
In the legend of the beautiful text....
Please don't let the smell of the cigarette leave the place language;
but before you limp to the sky, think well.
because, I'm used to the absence;
your panting face behind the whiteness;
help me with a love sonnet to trim my poems and that's enough,
every night letters ask me:

where have I lost my words??
tell him.... :

you are an apple stolen from the coat of Eve;
if a beautiful dream surprised you
I will give it my wings....
to get out from the injured white poetry,

so give me your hands to dream,
I'm still luring the beloved songs to wear you.
You were together running and sweating in the future glass,
we were milking the moon together,
and in the memory there is a rose and a pen;
the tree is a woman feeds her brushes with anthem
drops to fill the questions,

then she stays to tell the story to the passengers
about how doves are dead….
come on, and light the speech oil,
because you are the probability of the coming hour,
to make the ears sleep on the wind pillow….
The nipples of the sun are elegant this morning,
Dribbling grapes, and injure the tree…..
I was like someone sits on the wind borders,
waiting a cloud, and then cries….
and me finally, I draw a wound on the water;
to walk alone proudly in the path of the story,
your bare voice surmounted in front of the ruin…
But, I fear losing my poems in your loneliness.
So wait for me….
I will come back before the whiteness by two nights and a kiss,
so give me your lips; to sleep…..

The word of fire

When the sunset saliva flowed on the night verge,
on the nipple of the sun was a naked tree.
Reflecting the face of Allah.
And on the other nipple was a lily from the galaxy lip.
You relate to the illusion a cloud.

So let me write a poem to the wind,
in a morning asking for a rose
Disclosing the clay when the absence sneaks into my face;
Poetry is the fire's words.
Leading to suicide on a bouquet of eternity thirst.
So let's establish a new death, in which poets are not dying.
When arguing with the poem ears.
Only words spoil the rest of our desire.
With a woman on a confusion palm.
A lily got tired of waiting   .
Please take the ink of the place, and get away from the poem
foretop.
We are the holes of our memories;
drenching our dreams with the dawn gasp.
We end up like a dream on a sleepy sob face …

He is the man that

Who said that dawn doesn't know him?
Yes… who has said that?
He is secreting night;
when the sunset flows to poem end;
the flute, which surrendered stealthily to the day song,
it runs away from the maze saliva,
and realized itself the strain of spectrum.
When he got purified from the spray of the distance…
Because when he begins to please the sea;
and whenever he listens to the braids of argument,
he does not rush to call out…
Then he releases the letters of destiny, obsessed by the idea of the
moon.
he was like that…
So he was seducing waves somewhere;

he walks with bare lips,
deceiving a star in the astonishment of stones,
which are heaped on the threshold of legends…..
He has no face if the star rigs the moon braids.
Stealthily; he dips his face in the top of the poem,
the biography of exile was his heartbreak,
and the wind was the questions' desire.
And in a pen's jar,
he forgot that he is encrusted with fire and wound colors.
Like a god surviving death sometimes,
and then leaves smiling to the havoc…

Hanging about in her eyes

He was delirious…
And writing the heart lip which is lying on a tree branch,
He was greater than the distance….
And then the metaphor.
He plants his words in the poetry cup to make leafy lines;
on the alabaster of gods.
Then he looks to the list of seduction on the border of a cloudy
balcony
amid the dream…
The tattoo which is hung on the nipples,
of the dream roils the questions mood   .
But could its fingers get lost in night breadth,
to create names for the coming trip…..??
His hands were invoking, and his fingers are set on dew .
Towards a star face;
holding evening in his eyes, and the fingers of the wind sing,
like a disaster counting its joys.
who told the night to get purified
we didn't finish our prayer yet…
We are still dipping our groans in the beginning of the desire.
Till the distance recovers from its dust;
and the clouds do not be confused,
we darned the clay speech so not to cry the inkwell;
then we throw our yearnings in the gap of leaving,
may be the night hangs around in her eyes.

As the rose night that know me

Sometimes I miss the absence,
as the rose night that know me…
I knead the tale of the clay veins,
I could stretch my poems, even light wind starting from fire…
Perfume of the waves coming from travels.
Like this…
Watering the night taxidermist; with the cloves
in the morning spinster.
But the sand stack;
the color of the day bathed, making a bone coal
earrings for the evening…
oh! resident revelation, inspire I give birth for a poem;
burning sense, bleeding of roses to be a kiss dripped
as a night of a word in the bosom of a star …
But the spice that travels dawn,
still collecting wind dune of words.

and then gathering up cloud,
to crucify the doves on my chest…
so, we left on the road our letters, and of the water pain
the sunset will tremble,
and under the tree…
It trims nails clouds…
We were walking, we didn't awaken the sleeping sky;
and the sun caressed **the**poem,

with the birds that burns water…
For you…
A kiss slapped the face of the wind,
her fingers exploded of longing;
and the night smiled.

Only for you…
The navel of the story is a god that gets laid with a letter.
And then planted a cloud in my words to burn the wind;
And suspends the distance on my lips, to greened whiteness…

How to Generate a poem?

I am like that,
when I stay alone…
The void got filled with me;
under a sky with honey and almonds.
Thus, I throw my face out of the window, to pick up letters,
and ask myself:

how to generate a poem?
and how exactly does it happen?
It is probably…
A shadow breathes misery;
while the smoke soars over the whiteness,
it travels a long way, and sings chants from the memory glass;
the poem is no more than an orphan girl in absence….
swept by an acid night,
and a sunset stranger than the idea of absence   .
She…
Her stabbed dreams are like a desperate star,
winnowing the infested rustiness;
but when the sun stretches on a butterfly face…

It will be sitting under the evening amulets,
mummifying the night with the moon honey.
and the sky is a cloud raining metaphor….

She is…
My haven in the face of words to become strange.

The absence alerts me to a beautiful death…
I was burning on a bosom of a bird, which taught me,
how to fly lonely on a branch of a tree!!
I grope a poem; in which the passengers' dreams become green.
I am still embroiling the roots of the trees to become a star,
my voice is the night of darkness.
Hurting the Moon and combing the story hair….
Weaver on the sun lips the details of the sunset…
But I am complaining from the rain of her lips.
when the absence bursts,
like questions in the eyes of a cat…
The moon annoys an apple hung on,
the wishes' questions;
with waves that taught the sea….
How to count its sunk people.
And here I am flying from one wave to a wave its navel is the sea
lips.
Counting the distance from the moon to her lips…
So a star comes out of my mouth, flying away to the question.
And asks me:
How to generate a poem….?
How does that happen eventually…?

A sky for a foreign bird

Nothing on your face reveals the turmoil hour.
The night asks you....   :
When can we set up our suitcases?
and embrace a tree that has said to its beloved:
"Let's burn a shameless kiss."
But the wind is courting a moon, joking the dice,
with a child leaves the school early....
The afterglow is drawing with its brush a lip
has shoed a water drop....
She was still painting a little prayer of a time dust;
and she is courting a peep on a vein mole.
For the rose to sleep with noise in her eyes;
and the afterglow is continuing in crying.

A magician drinking a cloud

He was looking at her,
from the suspended hole in the sky.
and whenever he enticed a color,
his hook trembles and get stained with dreams,
when he impales his lips in the whiteness.
How much was he afraid of nudity in writing??
But whenever he starts to write bare lips,
He puts a teapot on his mouth to kindle a poem
Then he expels the wind which came late.
The night was falling like a teen cloud;
Bold like autumn, and its night wet with twilight and almonds   .
Her turquoise shirt is a magician drinking a coffee, and looking at
her legs......
while she's hiding grass between two silk palms.
and with the intensity of admiration, he was hammering her laugh
nail
in the story wood....
He cries and says :

O, storm .... hug me, to get used to my silence,
this purple neck does not say trivialities,
but the wind has a lie that is believed by the evening...
We were flying and the lightning rhythm was our lust.
Lonely, I was swimming in the night of solitude and loss.
As if the spray that draws the sadness at dawn;
rises with chants to make a cloud with it.
This cloud flies with two honey wings...

A balcony on high whiteness

There…. on that whiteness;
It's enough for the poem which is full of void milk to get wet.
But every night the silence returns to its mother,
and the clay as usual leaves the water to the insomnia dawn;
purifying stealthily to do the cloud pray;
but when death travels, light stems from her lips;
She was beautiful like the travel of places.
Every morning, she disperses ears for the wine evenings;
and for the dawn coming from faraway, tapping the lust wheat,
for the night overlooking the question…
O…… full of what looks like absence,
embroider your language with the henna of far distances,
to let the twilight leak into the shadows.
I will plant the rose of the salt from the night vaccine;
so knead your pride with the sunset water;
before bursting the water language ….
but who can save you from the clay groan??
You will be alone planting grass in your expatriation bosom.
Then do not approach the poem;
perhaps the wind can rat on you,
and the flute surrenders to sleep with the sea…
Because whenever a star got stuck between your lips;
I get a cloud in my moneybox, to provoke the void.
To buy the rain .

Teach me how to drown in the absence!!

She didn't sleep....
But she woke up frightened by the hiss of her desire;
And when she knew that the flute is fond of leaving;
She assigned some words to the wound,
then she combed the poem hair…
and embroidered a (Borda) for the wind.
the bunches of water were falling bereaved
from the impact of the anthem.
So vow me some of the poem;
And don't pass a texture on the fireplace of the heart.
Night taught me drowning in the absence…
She glimpses the lightning image behind the dream.
Splintering into his loneliness that is full of dew.
At the beginning of night, she hung the sunset on the lust of stones;
so as not the huskiness of the evening tears her fingers…
And I stream lonely in the darkness of my blood;
to release the dawn lips.
then run like a little boy in the day basket,
behind the kids laugh;
I expel my lips to let sleep the story"M "…

A night invades my pillow

I saw her on a pile of my discarded dreams,
Sleeps on the memory of the trees as a night
invades my pillow…
She walks on her nipples, they are trickling anthem.
The night did not sing…
But saddled pregnant distances;
to knead her lips with almonds and clouds.
On the night of ruins how overlies her brows.
But you do not know what happens,
while the sea surrendered to me??
Gypsy virgin desperate in a lonely night….
Only the sun gets rid to the lightning;
to bloom the salt surprise.
But when the tale is Haunted a pain; I kiss the wind
to smell wave…..
And there…..
On the beach, I comb my blood.
The moon passes rambler on the sand,

but I didn't shot for him any attention…
Didn't you see two orphans' stars bombing on your chest?
Whenever blooms the virgin night,
You come back invoking the power quest.
Since, I visited your eyes the night don't know me;
The revelation lose one's marbles,

And the torrent did not expect the exile language,
until you realized my window,
then you lock the dark night in my blood,
and you shake in the speech nest my story;
and finally you realize that the disappeared dove.
That I have taken on my hand on my shoulder.
And you kindled in the night of resurrection my pain;
turned my face for that knows me,
and I held my eyebrows as the term......
I stayed to restore her laugh on my face
with a wait as water ...
to me, a cache of dream hanging on her lips,
to me, I narrate for her what happened;
while the sea surrendered me.....

And you hide the night into a poem

Me and the night…..
Us two; we don't have a friend.
Only the light is spelling grain of chocolate;
We eat it piece by piece; and then we throw
the bones of the poem to exiles…
then the distance does not leave us,
even aging fingernails , for uprooting the maze.
I don't have the clouds only one metaphor to her lips.
to stay up late on a mine and a confusion…..
every night the cloud cries its night when;
the speech stays away from the memory.
So…..
myths cry a story threw its bags for
the first train, before ten o'clock in the night.

But howtobend lightning to capture a mole falls
accidentally in the view of the dream?

to make the night empty from its silk.
The wind ventures with a rainy night,
looks to the letters from a jealousy butterfly.
Then we decide to sleep on the rope of the poem.
We count our fingers with fear
of the afar expatriation.
Then say…… Amin

we are not satisfied of the night soul,
and we were not vacuuming our scorpions pains.
O… doves come back to me where we are lonely
from our evil of our love….
And from the evil of the nostalgia topless…..

Say…… Amin,

nothing in its place; when the wind violated your face.
And you hide the night in a poem;
sleep lonely on a fragment dream,
in the vision body…..

I will call you the poem

My love, how much is beautiful;
When I commit suicide, in a rosy way,
Yes like that…
like a cigarette in the mouth of a sailor,
but I don't have a more beautiful way,
I flow lonely like milk on the sun verge,
I hang up my bygone face at the roof of maze,
then I let my breath to the chance,
as if I'm making our night a story for passengers;
I don't know how can I do this ?
but I persist to go far away to the no….. thing….
I fight with poets to write you in a form of a sob, for example.
Yes…..
I'm dreaming and waiting for your sudden coming like the rain of
spring….
maybe, I will give you a name but what name??
words are coming back to their nests at the end of the evening.
My confusion is to write the face of the void amid the dream,

a hidden perfume discloses your absence;
because I still miss you.
Like an herb smell….
Like an exile perfume…..
Like a color of rain….
I close my eyes and answer the eldest questions of the sun
I wish a cup of coffee on your nipples….
to sleep with the shy sweat on the whiteness' pores

and I'm behind the twilight seeing the wind creates
a song like a nonfinite verb
but how can your night
be silent at the last star to let me run away?
we were eating the moon like an almond grain.....
when I weave from your looks agates,
for the neck of the evening;
you were my star lover who dips its feet into the river.
And the moon is single, flirts the stars to stay there,
guarding the kisses' brook.
O... I can't stand the noise of nipples;
which sweeps away the nude moment.
I was running away from you....
from the sadness satiety......
Confused like an upset dress
on your perfumed body with the moon henna,
my throat obliges the voices to the exile of term,
to pass my blood treason, I call the things by their names.
And I call you finally the Poem...

Jerk from an old wound

I'm extremely bad…
Yes….
I'm bad somehow.
But I'm not bad as you can imagine.
All poems know me, and my compass is the wind hands;
the flute has the place frontiers, and your eyes have the water joy;
get away a little bit from me; I will hide confusion in my pocket.
And share my pain in the rustle of roses,
so give me a wine as a present to let lovers drink.
Each night; I was emptying the story in your voice.
to feed the wind the moon fruit…
So don't leave to the water concerns
your lips are like streaming rivers,
so let's sit and drink our desire's coffee.
But don't say that I am so bad………
The sadness is flying alone in the deep night.
Putting a laugh in a cigarette made from the absence breathes.
And I am….
No longer care about you,
when you shed a coffee from your eyes each morning,
because, I am strange without noise in the marble…
As you think…

Kid of lightning

She's just a woman....
I will hang her face on the wall until the gravel gets burnt;
that's why I don't respond,
to her whining when she smokes...
her eyes are sitting on a bench, drinking a coffee
the evening is sad...
she was taming her fingers in the deep question,
and I am usually stupid like a matchstick....
full of my silliness...
the shade and the whiteness' insane people are conspiring against
me,
but what does lure me, is the dream in the joints of the absence,
because I have never seen in my life a cigarette puts lipsticks;
and lures poets....
my nose is not breathing well,
but went out for a walk in the neighbors' yard.
It knows the secrets of seduction,
and ignores the intentions of the clouds...
The wind takes off its clothes and went to bed,
then it hung its beauty in the cloud ear....

like the kid of lightning or more seduction;
and doesn't care about its kisses which are dumped amid the poem,
the tree that starves at the night between
dawn and its eyes,
is cutting the nails of letters;
the clouds sign dreams for the swarm of neglected balconies......
and the twilight is some of its lost flavor,
and this sky with cracked hands like my old Grandma,
on which I hang my mustache on the distances of its childhood,
then I sort a maze, streaming like the saliva of faraway distances;
a seller for exiles;
I was falling like a drop of drunken sweat.
From a shivering cheek insists to cry......
Taking off its fingers;
when the water knocks the anthem doors;
and asks the absence .... :

Not to get drunk alone, and to be kind with the bunches....

She didn't say anything

She….. didn't say anything,
but she was seducing the wind compass,
then she burnt a poem on my eyebrow……
she was waiting for me,
and writing a speech for the coming storms;
every night, I look for my story
dodging like a rider who lost the dove way….
our kisses had the taste of the wind.
When I received her hands,
and focused on the language of estrangement.
I asked the wind:
If her shadow has come back before the dawn looking for me?
to weep the twilight that is called…… the absence,
to forget me like a perfume bottle……

Tell her…..
the sadness in my city is a piece of chocolate,
eaten by children before the sunset leave,
no, it's not your face that over talked,
it was praying alone on the wine….
And the rain milk was dropping from the wind nipples.
So give me an ear, to ask the twilight:
Why does it not wake up early??
and let the speech on a cooker,
bleed like a cunning candle.

Spray full of silence

The dream that overlies your voice,
was the last bunch, when the moon was not able to scream,
just before the morning;
we see from there......
A coming light from the upper distance;
comes out from the throat of a patient star.....
The winged sky drinks its noise from the cups of rain.
It put out the star lamps, to let the galaxy sleep.
But despite the reflection of colors, the cloud still dangled;

It took off its shoes in a spray flavor full with silence......
it knew very well that there is no form in the sky;
but, the sun fingers hung on nipples dripping with poetry,
and the stars are sleeping.....

For the beautiful smile

He used to say her name, in winter and summer trip
No voice but the sun face.
Living in a bird lung,
and lighting stealthily forests in the clouds
(The Nawassi) was crying of the stupid poets' dreams.
He does not know how to read the grass;
but he listens to the trivialities of the sadness,
walking in the tone of erasure,
and do not realize the night of its fingers.
And from its acid dawn,
he stretches his body that is wet of love,
on the body map.
and (the Nawassi) is still rumbling
in the market of significance.
he was looking for a thread to tie the wine with the face of a poem;
but he found nothing more than naïve tales.......

However, the beautiful smile has another story.
he was washing the night and putting it on a confused dish;
silently, and does not disturb the wind till the doves sleep.
Tired, with no place but her eyes.....
And in the womb of metaphor, he makes her lips a pot of incense.

I told him to:
Stone its slaves with seven poems
And run away from the coming storms.

And then open your distances to a yawning rose,
With confusion in its names.
the wind is showering to let a star grow in the bottom of the story;
and make the bed to let the whiteness sleep.

He...... never complied with the cloud.
Thus, he left alone to the (Sidra) of water.
Gasping with love;
and waiting for the night to come.

Don't worry

They ask you about wind children;
tell them, they are what the clay secretes
from the beginnings of the salt;
your face is haunted by infatuation....
you were more beautiful than the berry leaves,
but I was not sure; I was standing at the end of the station
waiting for something,
all passengers have come back;
except your eyes missed the moon appointments
and, I have told the absence to slow down.......
like a fire flower, the speech get burnt when I smell you.
Something in your face is enough to make the wine die,
so rearrange your lips.
The coffee is a virgin sprawling in a beautiful morning.

It was enough to drink it....
Or to flirt it like an old drunkard,
You were the poem I have completed before autumn
Went by on my balcony......
And people who conceal the revelation on your navel, have not argued,
But they wrote poetry from the mood of gods,
So fill me with poetry from the lung of poem....
to pour water languages,
and light in the context all letters
....

Every night lovers don't leave my minaret,
Then I choose a place there; in the ends of the will,
So prepare as much as you could of kisses for me…..
and don't worry; I will tell your eyes on the day of the meeting.

Publisher's list

If you have enjoyed *Sky For Foreign Bird* consider these other fine books from Mwanaka Media and Publishing:

Cultural Hybridity and Fixity by Andrew Nyongesa
The Water Cycle by Andrew Nyongesa
Tintinnabulation of Literary Theory by Andrew Nyongesa
I Threw a Star in a Wine Glass by Fethi Sassi
South Africa and United Nations Peacekeeping Offensive Operations by Antonio Garcia
Africanization and Americanization Anthology Volume 1, Searching for Interracial, Interstitial, Intersectional and Interstates Meeting Spaces, Africa Vs North America by Tendai R Mwanaka
A Conversation…, A Contact by Tendai Rinos Mwanaka
A Dark Energy by Tendai Rinos Mwanaka
Africa, UK and Ireland: Writing Politics and Knowledge Production Vol 1 by Tendai R Mwanaka
Best New African Poets 2017 Anthology by Tendai R Mwanaka and Daniel Da Purificacao
Keys in the River: New and Collected Stories by Tendai Rinos Mwanaka
Logbook Written by a Drifter by Tendai Rinos Mwanaka
Mad Bob Republic: Bloodlines, Bile and Crying Child by Tendai Rinos Mwanaka
How The Twins Grew Up/Makurire Akaita Mapatya by Milutin Djurickovic and Tendai Rinos Mwanaka
Writing Language, Culture and Development, Africa Vs Asia Vol 1 by Tendai R Mwanaka, Wanjohi wa Makokha and Upal Deb

Zimbolicious Poetry Vol 1 by Tendai R Mwanaka and Edward Dzonze
Zimbolicious: An Anthology of Zimbabwean Literature and Arts, Vol 3 by Tendai Mwanaka
Under The Steel Yoke by Jabulani Mzinyathi
A Case of Love and Hate by Chenjerai Mhondera
Epochs of Morning Light by Elena Botts
Fly in a Beehive by Thato Tshukudu
Bounding for Light by Richard Mbuthia
White Man Walking byJohn Eppel
A Cat and Mouse Affair by Bruno Shora
Sentiments by Jackson Matimba
Best New African Poets 2018 Anthology by Tendai R Mwanaka and Nsah Mala
Drawing Without Licence by Tendai R Mwanaka
Writing Grandmothers/Escribiendo sobre nuestras raíces:Africa Vs Latin America Vol 2 by Tendai R Mwanaka and Felix Rodriguez
The Scholarship Girl by Abigail George
Words That Matter by Gerry Sikazwe
The Gods Sleep Through It by Wonder Guchu
The Ungendered by Delia Watterson
The Big Noise and Other Noises by Christopher Kudyahakudadirwe
Tiny Human Protection Agency by Megan Landman

Soon to be released
Ghetto Symphony by Mandla Mavolwane
Of Bloom Smoke by Abigail George
*Denga reshiri yokunze kwenyika*by Fethi Sassi
A Portrait of Defiance by Tendai Rinos Mwanaka

Nationalism: (Mis)Understanding Donald Trump's Capitalism, Racism, Global Politics, International Trade and Media Wars, Africa Vs North America Vol 2 by Tendai R Mwanaka

Ashes by Ken Weene and Umar O. Abdul

Ouafa and the Thawra: About a Lover From Tunisia by Arturo Desimone

Thoughts Hunt The Loves/Pfungwa dzinovhima Vadiwa by Jeton Kelmendi

When Escape Becomes the only Lover by Tendai R Mwanaka

https://facebook.com/MwanakaMediaAndPublishing/

Printed in the United States
By Bookmasters